A Story Within

Abbey Gelner

A Story Within

With Proverbs Woman Publishing.

Cover Designed by Abbey Gelner

ISBN- 979-8-9942657-4-1

Contents

Chapter 1

Where My Story Begins

Some stories begin long before we realize they are being written.

Chapter 1

Where My Story Begins

My story begins more than thirty-five years ago, when I was a preschooler and my mom, just thirty-two years old, was diagnosed with breast cancer.

Most children remember playgrounds and birthday parties. Sleepovers with friends. Mother-daughter afternoons filled with small traditions that become lifelong memories. They remember scraped knees being kissed to feel all better, and bedtime stories read in steady voices. They aren't in the moment hoping for more moments just like this. They are simply just living and assuming there will always be more time.

What I remember are cancer treatment centers and hospital rooms.

I remember the weight of hours spent curled up on a cold wooden chair beside my mom as she received chemotherapy. My legs would dangle and swing because the height of a child didn't quite reach the floor. The air in those rooms always felt too still, thick with the sharp sting of antiseptic, a smell that would become all too familiar. The walls were sterile white, the kind that didn't offer comfort or distraction. Machines hummed and beeped steadily, marking time in heartbeats and medication drips. Reminding us how fragile life really is.

I remember nights spent in her hospital room, sleeping on a narrow cot tucked in the corner. I would pull the thin blanket up to my chin and close my eyes, wishing we were home. Wishing the smell of disinfectant would turn back into the smell of dinner simmering on the stove or laundry fresh being folded from the dryer. Closing my eyes while envisioning I was laying peacefully in my pink canopy bed on the second floor of our home. I remember pretending to sleep while listening to the rhythm of machines and the soft murmur of nurses checking vitals. Even then, I think I understood the inevitable.

The short time we were at home, I remember watching my mom try to smile through nausea and exhaustion. She worked hard to make things feel normal for us. She still wrote out Christmas lists in perfect cursive, making sure my brothers and I received equal gifts. Even when her body was weak, she made sure the magic stayed intact. I can still see her handwriting so balanced and thoughtful. She was losing strength, but she never lost intention. She knew her time with us was limited. And still, she made the most of it.

Her unwavering love, her soft smile, her memorable laughter followed by her well-known "shhhhsh," forever etched into the hearts of those lucky enough to know her. Her illness did not take her spirit or her tenderness, and it certainly did not take her determination or love she had for all of us. She continued to hold her head high even when the weight of the world was on her.

Then there was the bathroom.

This is where silent battles were held. Where I watched her cry as strands of her hair collected at the bottom of the bathtub. The water would drain slowly, pulling soft wisps toward the silver circle at the bottom. It wasn't dramatic. It wasn't loud. It was quiet.

A quiet surrender she tried so hard to hide from us.

I don't remember asking questions. I don't remember touching the hair or reaching for her. I remember standing still, watching her. I remember the sound of the water spiraling down. I remember the silence between us and I remember her horizontal scar across her chest where the cancer invaded her.

Even then, I think part of me understood something was slipping away. As a child, you don't articulate fear. You absorb it.

The most vivid memory I can recall is one summer afternoon on our three acres of plush green lawn. The sky was impossibly blue, the kind of blue that feels endless. The sun was warm against my skin, almost like a hug. Birds chirped in the trees. It was one of those perfect, ordinary days that should have blended into the background of childhood.

My mom sat with my two older brothers and me. I remember her voice, steady but soft, as she said, “I won’t be here with you for long…”

And in that instant, the perfect day shattered.

Everything that had felt warm and safe suddenly felt heavy. The sounds of birds and wind faded. The warmth of the sun turned distant. I don’t remember the words that came after that. I don’t remember if she explained, reassured, or tried to prepare us.

I stopped listening.

My guards went up instantly. Even as a child, I must have known that if I let the rest of her words in, something inside me would break open. So, I did what felt safest, I shut down. I stared at the grass. I focused on the sky. I let her voice blur into the background.

Back then, shutting down felt like control. If I didn’t listen to the words, maybe they wouldn’t become reality.

Now, decades later, I would give anything to remember what she said next. I have replayed that moment countless times in my mind, trying to fill in the missing pieces. I can only imagine the love and advice she must have poured into us and the courage it took for her to speak those words out loud.

At eleven years old, the fragile world I knew finally shattered.

At thirty-nine years old, my mom fearlessly took God's hand and left us for her home in eternity. There were no dramatic last words etched into my memory. No cinematic goodbye. Just a quiet understanding that the chapter we had been living in for years had finally closed. Even though she was no longer hurting and she was made whole again in a way her earthly body never could be, there is a part of me that still feels selfish for wishing there had been more time.

More birthdays. More conversations. More afternoons on the lawn. More of her voice.

I don't remember the days immediately after in detail. I only remember pieces. I remember our entire house being engulfed with colorful flowers. I overheard the hushed conversations and the whispers as I would pass by. Casseroles lined our countertops for weeks in an effort to feed our family. I remember adults telling me I was strong.

I wasn't strong. I was quiet.

People told us she was no longer suffering and that she was in a better place. I wanted to believe that, but what I felt most clearly was the shift. I felt the absence and the way something that was so steady had been removed from beneath my feet. They tried to comfort me with their words, but what they couldn't tell me was how to live in a place where she wasn't.

After a loss, there is an abundance of support. As quickly as the house fills with people, the meals appear. Voices remain soft and for a while, you are surrounded. Then slowly, life resumes. School continues and schedules return. The world moves forward, but you are left standing in a space that no longer feels like yours.

And it was within that moment that something began inside me.

It wasn't loud or dramatic. It was a quiet learning to hold things in. I began managing my emotions carefully, tightly and privately. It felt like something that needed to be contained. I believed that if I could control myself, maybe the rest of my world wouldn't come undone.

I didn't have the language for anxiety or depression. I didn't even know what grief was or how it was processed in a healthy way. I only knew that life had changed in a way I could not control. So, I quietly began to try to control myself.

Looking back now, I can see that this was likely where my mental health story began. Not in a dramatic collapse, but in a quiet tightening inside a little girl who believed being strong meant staying composed. I began to believe that if I could control myself, my emotions, my reactions, and my needs, then maybe I could protect what was left.

During this time, and for what I thought was a favor for everyone else, I didn't fall apart and I learned how to look fine. And for a long time, that would be enough.

Somewhere in that same season, I made a promise to myself. Someday, when I was older, I would find a way to honor my mom. I didn't know how and I didn't know when. I didn't even know what it would look like. But I felt it.

That promise was born out of loss and quiet determination not to let her story end with illness. It would follow me into every chapter that came next. What I didn't realize was that learning to look fine would shape those chapters just as much as that promise did.

This is where my story truly begins.

Chapter 2
Everything Was Fine

Childhood changes the moment innocence meets loss.

Chapter 2

Everything Was Fine

From the outside, everything was fine.

School resumed quickly, as if grief were something that could be scheduled around. My dad's work hours returned to normal. My brothers and I went back to classrooms, locker rooms, and homework at the kitchen table. The world did what it always does after tragedy, it kept moving.

People stopped lowering their voices when I walked into a room. The sympathetic tilts of heads softened into half-turned smiles as I would pass by. Teachers no longer paused when they said my name, just at the same time that the casseroles disappeared and the flowers wilted. The kitchen that was once filled with care and concern soon turned back into what it once was. Only this time my mom wasn't there. Her absence filled the air.

But life settled back into routine and so did I.

I went to sleepovers at friends' houses and laughed when I was supposed to laugh. I stood in the dim, stuffy basements of our church during middle school dances, taking in songs that felt far more important than they actually were. I tried hard not to be the emotional girl who had just lost her mom.

I didn't want to be fragile. I didn't want to be different. I didn't want to be pitied.

So I adjusted.

I had a core group of friends, the kind of friendships that fill cafeterias and hallways. The ones that also had Friday night plans. I was a friend to everyone. Often seen as easygoing, agreeable and dependable. But even when surrounded by people, I often felt slightly removed. It was like I was standing just outside the circle, always looking in and feeling slightly left out. There wasn't that one best friend I confided in fully and now that my mom was gone, there wasn't anyone at home I could fully confide in either.

At home, I quietly tried to step into a role I wasn't ready for. I told myself I was helping. I tried to be the "woman of the house," as if that were something an eleven-year-old could become simply by willing it. I folded laundry without being asked. I cleaned up dishes before they sat too long. I tried to anticipate needs before they were spoken and I ignored the needs of my own.

It felt productive. It felt responsible. It felt like control.

My dad worked hard during the day to provide for us, and I convinced myself that the least I could do was make things easier on him. I didn't want him to worry about me. I didn't want to add to the weight he was already carrying. The truth is, I needed him more than I let on, but needing someone meant acknowledging what was missing. So, instead I chose to remain capable. I chose to remain quiet. I chose to be fine.

After a few years had passed, my dad slowly stepped back into the dating world.

At first, I didn't know how to feel about that. The idea of it felt strange and unfamiliar. It was like something that didn't quite belong in the life we had rebuilt, but when the introductions began I was surprised by my own reaction. I actually enjoyed it.

We would get together with these new friends, most of them single parents navigating their own versions of loss or change. There were other kids my age and it felt like a family again when we would sit around backyard fire pits or gather in living rooms while the adults talked late into the evening. Laughter returned to our house in a way that felt lighter than the quiet we had grown used to.

For the first time in a long time, it didn't feel like everything revolved around what we had lost.

It felt normal. And I wanted normal more than anything.

I liked seeing my dad smile in a way that wasn't forced. I liked watching him relax. There was comfort in knowing he might not always carry the weight alone.

But even in the fun, there was a part of me that stayed cautious. I had already learned how quickly life could change.

So, while I laughed and made new friends, I also remained unsure. I often questioned how much of myself I could safely invest in others. I told myself not to get too attached to anyone new. I had become good at protecting what was left of my heart and what was left in our family.

Eventually, one relationship lasted longer than the others.

Slowly, what began as casual dinners and shared weekends turned into something more permanent. When my dad remarried, I told myself it was a good thing. He deserved happiness. We all did. And in many ways, it was good.

But there is something complicated about watching another woman step into a space your mother once held, even when no one is trying to replace her.

I think part of me hoped, quietly and without saying it out loud, that she might see me. Not just as another child in the house, but as a little girl who had lost her mom. I didn't need her to be my mother. I just needed someone to notice the absence.

Maybe she thought she was doing enough. Maybe navigating this new blended life was hard on her too. Maybe she believed space was what I needed. I don't actually know because nothing was ever discussed.

What I do know is that I learned once again to keep my feelings to myself.

I didn't talk about the tension I felt when things became uneasy, or the small ways that certain moments hurt. I didn't say how much I missed having someone who felt unquestionably "mine." Over time, I felt myself becoming a little quieter in my own home.

Like many teenage girls discovering the weight of disappointment, I slowly adjusted my expectations. It teaches you not to ask for too much. I had already learned how to manage my feelings carefully, and this felt no different.

Suppers at home slowly transitioned into suppers around my friends' kitchen tables. It was where I could feel a sense of belonging and a sense of home. Their homes felt warm and predictable. Their mothers asked questions and lingered in the doorway just a little longer. I would sit at their kitchen counters and soak in the normalcy of it all, the noise, the smells, the easy conversation. It is where I looked like I was fine.

It wasn't that I wanted a different family. I didn't. I just wanted to feel anchored somewhere. At my friends' houses, I felt that for a while. It was easier there. It was easier to laugh, it was easier to talk, and it was easier to blend in. It was easier to look like I was fine.

As middle school gave way to high school, something else began to grow in me.

High school became a season of motion.

Practices before and after school. Weeknight games and weekend tournaments. Homework spread across the kitchen table late into the night. Loud laughter in crowded hallways. Football games under our small town stadium lights where everything felt bigger than it probably was.

I had friendships that filled my weekends and inside jokes that carried us through the week. There were bonfires, barn loft movie nights, and conversations that felt urgent in the way only teenage conversations can.

By senior year, I found myself on the homecoming court, something that would have felt impossible to the little girl who once sat quietly in hospital rooms. I smiled for pictures with my friends, our arms wrapped around each other as if time wasn't already slipping forward. We gathered on the dance floor, soaking in every last moment Denver High School was giving us. The music played loudly, the lights too bright, and it felt like life was unfolding just like it should.

From the outside, it didn't just look fine, it looked like I had it all together.

It looked like I was thriving.

And in many ways, I was. I was living the high school teenage girl dream. Friends, dating, and sports filled my social calendar.

Soccer gave me something solid to pour myself into. I ran hard. I trained harder. I liked knowing that effort equaled results. There was comfort in that. There were rules and structure. There were wins you could measure and coaches that were proud of every win along the way. Achievement felt predictable and predictable felt safe.

Scholarship offers arrived. Out-of-state opportunities opened doors I hadn't even imagined walking through. Teachers encouraged me. Coaches believed in me. And my dad was proud of me.

He stood on the side lines with his hands on his hips, scanning the field like he was part of the game himself. He tried not to miss much. After games, he would replay the highlights with me and point out the moments I didn't even realize mattered. The extra effort and the quiet leadership I took on as captain of the team. The plays that didn't make the number on the scoreboard change but still changed the game. He saw things in me I was still learning to see in myself.

When the time came to choose what was next, I had options that would have taken me far from home. But I knew I was going to stay.

At the time, I told people it was practical. That it felt right. That it made sense financially, even though scholarship offers sat neatly stacked on my nightstand next to my bed.

What I didn't say was that I wasn't ready to be that far from him.

After losing my mom, my world had already shifted once in a way I couldn't control. My dad had become my steady place and that was my proof that something could remain.

Leaving felt like risking too much. So, I planned to build my future close to home.

As the high school years started to come to a close, there were final games and practices, and we wished there were more to follow. Lots of late-night conversations about what comes next. There was young love that felt certain at the time, friendships that felt permanent, and plans that felt within reach.

But more than anything, there was my dad.

He was in the stands with his unforgettable smile. He was in the driveway waiting for me to come home, always letting me know when I pushed my curfew to the limit, but never following through with any sort of punishment. He was at the kitchen table when I spread out scholarship letters and acceptance forms. He was steady.

After losing my mom, I had learned how quickly the ground could shift beneath you. So when I found something that felt solid, I held onto it.

Staying close wasn't about fear. It was about loyalty and about love that I felt within my family. It was about knowing that some anchors are worth protecting. For the first time in a long time, life didn't feel fragile. It felt full. And in that fullness, I believed we had found our rhythm again.

And for a while, it felt like everything was unfolding exactly the way it was supposed to.

Chapter 3

Daddy's Girl

The simplest moments often become the ones that matter the most.

Chapter 3

Daddy's Girl

To know my dad was to love him.

He was the kind of man who would pull over to help someone change a tire. The kind who would fix things before you even realized they were broken. He would buy something simply because it sparked a new interest, diving in fully and enthusiastically. At one point, thousands of fishing lures hung neatly across the spare bedroom walls, a collection that grew thanks to his newfound love of eBay. Each one represented the possibility, "just one more cast," or another quiet morning on the water.

He didn't talk much about what he carried inside, but you could see it in the way he showed up.

He was a friend to everyone. He believed in living life fully. His job was just that, a job. He didn't chase overtime or titles. Instead of extra hours at work, he would rather be on his boat at sunrise, casting his line into still water, content in the quiet rhythm of it. He would wait patiently for the tip of his rod to bend toward the water, hoping for a trophy bass to take the lure, and when one finally did, he would reel it in with the excitement of a child, admire it for a moment, kiss it gently, and toss it right back in. That was just who he was. He loved the anticipation of the catch, but he never needed to keep it.

When time allowed, he would take me with him. And he never missed the opportunity for our yearly trip up to northern Minnesota, to Lake Kabetogama. That week felt sacred. Predictable in the best way. The same cabin and the same early mornings. The same quiet stretch of water waiting for us. I never cared much about the fish. I didn't study the lures or pay attention to the technique. I sat in the boat for the ride. For the warmth of the sun on my skin and the gentle rock of the water beneath us. For the quiet company.

We didn't always talk much out there. We didn't need to. The silence wasn't heavy, it was comfortable. It allowed for the sound of the line casting out over the water and the hum of the motor to be enough. I would lean back and let the day unfold slowly, knowing there was nowhere else either of us needed to be.

He fished for the thrill of the catch. I went for him.

He understood something I wouldn't grasp until much later. Life was meant to be lived, not stockpiled. He was a child at heart, and his heart was pure gold.

If he wasn't on the boat fishing, he was on his Harley Davidson, taking in the sights around him. He loved the open road the same way he loved open water. The steady hum beneath him and the wind against his face. The feeling of movement without urgency. He didn't ride to get somewhere faster. He rode because it made him feel alive. He chased freedom in simple ways. Not by escaping life, but by fully living it.

He carried pride in his Native American heritage, a quiet reverence woven into who he was. And with this, he had a particular love for crows. Not everyone understands crows, but he did. He would stop at McDonald's just to buy a large order of french fries, roll down the window, and toss them out into the empty open grass. Within seconds, they would gather, black wings cutting across the sky, descending around him like old friends. He watched them with contentment, often telling me someday he wanted to fly.

When he wasn't chasing fish or riding into the wind, you could find him at home with his beloved chocolate lab, Hank, never far from his side. Wherever one was, the other was close behind.

There is something to be said about a man and his dog. About loyalty that doesn't need to be explained. About quiet companionship that fills the room without asking anything in return.

I'm not sure who needed who more. My dad needed his dog, or his dog that needed him.

Hank followed him from room to room, resting at his feet like it was his job to keep watch. And maybe in some ways, it was. Hank was there in the still moments and the moments where words weren't necessary. My dad loved deeply, even when he didn't always say much.

And Hank knew it.

Being the youngest and the only daughter in the house with two older brothers meant one thing, I was spoiled. But it was in the quiet ways that mattered the most. Not with extravagant things, but with attention and the small privileges that I pretended not to notice. He was overprotective and looked at me in a way that felt both proud and gentle at the same time. Being his daughter felt safe.

He was always proud of me. No matter what.

It didn't depend on wins on the field, awards or milestones. It wasn't tied to scholarships or homecoming courts. He was proud of the small things. The effort I gave and the way I carried myself. He was proud of the choices I made, and even when I doubted myself, he didn't.

The years after high school filled quickly. I attended college close to home. A young marriage that brought new responsibilities. He walked me down the aisle, smiling in that familiar way that made me feel both grown and still entirely his little girl.

And then he became Grandpa.

I watched a different kind of pride settle over him the first time he held my son, his first and only grandson. He stared at him, content and full of awe, as if memorizing every detail. Soon he was telling him about the memories they would make together. Fishing trips and future plans. Adding in harmless trouble only a grandpa and grandson could share.

When my daughter was born, he held her just as carefully, just as proudly. He looked at her the way he had always looked at me, proud before there was anything to prove. Seeing him with my children felt like watching life circle back on itself.

Life kept unfolding.

While on the phone our conversations could last a lifetime. He was never in a hurry to hang up. Even when there was nothing left to say, we would both linger, stretching out the silence just a little longer, neither of us wanting to be the first to say goodbye.

And he was always the first one to tell me happy birthday. No matter the time. No matter what he had going on. My phone would ring or buzz before anyone else had the chance. It became something I counted on without even realizing I was counting on it.

That was just who he was.

Steady. Intentional. Present.

With him, I never questioned my worth.

Chapter 4
The Phone Call

Life can change direction without warning.

Chapter 4

The Phone Call

"Abbey, Dad was just killed."

My brother's voice was unlike anything I had ever heard before. Then, silence. It pressed in around me as I fell to my knees outside my night microbiology class, a prerequisite I was taking for nursing school.

For a few moments, I stayed there on the floor. Time had no shape. The hallway looked the same. The lights hummed. Someone's footsteps echoed in the distance.

And then something inside me shifted and I stood up.

My legs felt unfamiliar, like they belonged to someone else. I brushed my hands against my jeans, as if that small movement could steady me. I gripped the cold doorknob and walked back into the classroom.

The fluorescent lights seemed brighter in there. My classmates sat at their desks, pens moving across paper, eyes fixed on the whiteboard. The professor was mid-sentence.

I waited until he paused.

"I have to go," I said.

My voice didn't shake the way I thought it might.

"My dad was just killed."

There are certain sentences you never imagine saying out loud. That was one of them. It felt like I was watching myself from somewhere else, as if a movie was playing and I had somehow become the main character.

The room went still. I don't remember what my professor said in response. I don't remember anyone looking at me. I only remember gathering my belongings and walking out.

Silence followed me down the hallway and out to the parking lot.

It was just past sunset. The last light had slipped below the horizon, and the sky was turning from its orange cast to black. The air had turned cool, the kind of chill that seeps through your clothes before you realize it's there. A light rain began to fall, barely noticeable at first. Just enough to leave small dark circles on the pavement. Leaves scraped across the sidewalk, pushed cautiously by the wind.

The campus looked the same as it always did. Cars lined up in neat rows. Streetlights casting yellow halos onto wet asphalt. Nothing about the sky suggested that my life had just fractured.

I stood there in it. Just ten days before my twenty-eighth birthday.

I had no intention of driving anywhere. I also had no intention of staying. Shock wrapped itself around me, heavy and numb. I climbed into the driver's seat and closed the door, shutting out the sound of the rain.

I remember thinking how ordinary everything looked. How the world kept moving even when mine had stopped. I sat there in silence as the rain grew heavier, streaking down my windshield.

And then the tears came.

I didn't call anyone. I don't remember reaching for my phone at all. I only remember sitting there, staring through the windshield as the rain grew heavier and the sky darkened around me. Staring into a new world that just separated me into a before and after.

A knock on my window pulled me back. I blinked and unlocked the door. The rush of cool air and rain met my face as I stepped out. Arms wrapped around me before I had the chance to say anything. I don't remember who held me first. I only remember the feeling of being steadied, as if my body might have given out without someone else anchoring it.

Voices moved around me in low tones. Plans were being made. Someone would drive. Someone would gather my things. Someone would make sure I got home. I stood in the middle of it all, listening but not fully absorbing. Everything felt distant, slightly removed, as if I were watching it unfold instead of living it.

The campus lights reflected off the wet pavement, and the world looked painfully ordinary. I remember thinking how strange it was that everything else continued. The sky was filled with a burst of a thousand stars. The ground remained firm beneath my feet. The world did not pause to acknowledge that mine had.

We drove to my house.

I don't remember much about the ride there. Somewhere between the parking lot and the driveway the details were given to me. It was a hit and run accident. He and his beloved chocolate lab, Hank, had been struck. The driver hadn't stopped to help him. She had called for help for herself instead. I remember streetlights passing in rhythm and the steady sound of tires against wet pavement. I remember staring out the window, watching the rain distort everything outside, as if the world had been smeared and softened.

The details kept coming.

The words landed harder than the first sentence had. It wasn't just that he was gone. It was how. It was the fact that he had been left there. His lifeless body in a ditch, covered with cornstalks in a way to cover up the scene. That fact that someone had seen him, known what they had done, but chose themselves.

I remember wrapping my arms around myself in an attempt to feel the relief of a hug. The rain blurred the road ahead of me, or maybe it was the tears. I cried in a way that felt unfamiliar. It was deep, guttural, and uncontrolled. Not the tears that you can wipe away and keep going. These were the kind that rise from somewhere beneath your ribs and force their way out.

As we drove, I began calling the people I wanted around me. The ones who felt safe. The ones who would not try to fix it or soften it but simply sit in it with me. I don't remember exactly what I said. I only remember repeating the sentence, over and over, as if saying it out loud might make it make sense.

"My dad was just killed."

The anger began before I even reached home. It wasn't explosive. It was sharp and precise. A tightening in my chest. A question that kept circling.

How could someone leave him there? He was the kind of man who would pull over for a stranger without hesitation. The kind who would give before being asked. A son. A father. A husband. A grandpa. A friend to all.

And someone chose to walk away.

The anger came fast, but it didn't come alone because underneath it was something heavier.

Now both of my parents were gone.

The sentence felt impossible to hold. I had already learned how to live without a mother. I had already done the quiet work of surviving one loss. And now, in the span of a phone call, I was standing in a world without either of them.

It wasn't just grief. It was abandonment layered on top of memory. It was the reopening of a wound I thought I had closed.

I was no longer someone who had lost a parent. I was someone who had lost both.

When we pulled into the driveway, the house looked the same as it had that morning. The porch light was on. The windows glowed warm from the inside. It felt almost offensive that it still stood there so normal.

My in-laws were already there. They stepped forward gently, their faces tight with concern, and without many words they gathered my kids into their arms. I remember the weight of that moment more than the details. Handing my children over felt both necessary and unbearable. I kissed their heads without speaking any words and I walked into the bathroom and locked the door behind me.

I sat on the floor with my back against the door, the cool tile grounding me in a way nothing else could. The house was full of quiet movement. Voices in the kitchen with that familiar tone. Footsteps in the hallway that seemed to pause outside the door. But I was on the inside of that small room and it felt contained. Manageable. I could control that space.

I called a few people. My aunt that lived across the street and one of my best friends. Neither asked any questions, they just came. Almost instantly.

Within minutes, the house filled with familiar faces and low voices.

But I refused to leave.

I refused to go to the accident scene. I refused to go to my dad and stepmom's house, where the rest of my family had gathered. I refused to see anything that would make this my new reality.

It was at that moment that I shut off the rest of the world.

I didn't want to allow myself to process the details. I didn't want to picture the ditch, the flashing emergency lights cutting through the night sky, or his body and Hank lying there in a place that felt so wrong. I could not step into a space that would confirm what my mind was still fighting to reject.

My dad was gone.

But, if I stayed where I was and I kept the door closed and the world out, maybe I could hold that truth at a distance just a little longer.

So, I stayed behind a locked door and let everyone else move around the reality I was not ready to face.

Chapter 5
The World Moves On

I was standing still while everything else kept moving.

Chapter 5

The World Moves On

The night my dad was killed, my world shut down.

Within fifteen hours of my dad being killed, I was sitting in a therapist's office being prescribed antidepressants.

The room was quiet. Calm. Intentionally so. The kind of space designed to soften hard conversations. There were tissues placed within reach and neutral artwork on the walls. A chair angled toward the couch I was sitting on in a way that suggested safety. I remember thinking how strange it was to be sitting there while the rest of my life felt like it was in pieces.

My employer meant well to send me there. Everyone meant well. I understand that now. They wanted to stabilize me to prevent what they feared might come next. But something in me recoiled at the idea of it.

How dare someone try to fix this?

Wasn't I supposed to feel devastated? My dad, my only living parent, had just been killed. Suddenly there were appointments, prescriptions and plans. It felt like I was being handed instructions for how to grieve. I wasn't ready for instructions, and I wasn't ready to be told how to feel.

It wasn't that I didn't believe in therapy. It was that I wasn't ready for grief to be managed.

The prescription felt like a quiet suggestion that this needed to be regulated. That my sadness needed boundaries and my anger should be softened. I did not want it softened. I did not want it organized. I wanted my dad back.

I left that office holding a bottle of medication in one hand and a reality I could not yet comprehend in the other. Everything felt procedural. As though my loss had already been categorized and assigned a treatment plan.

In the beginning people showed up. They filled the house. They brought food. They sat in the living room and spoke in lowered voices. They hugged me tightly and told me how sorry they were. All of the same things that I remember after losing my mom. Except this time, I didn't feel like I had anyone to turn to. When my mom died, I still had my dad. There was still someone to call. Someone older. Someone steady. Now it felt like there wasn't anyone.

In the days that followed, there were arrangements to be made, court dates to attend, statements to give, and questions that no one could answer. There were police reports and insurance forms that felt both clinical and hollow. They spoke about timelines and procedures, about evidence and processing. They used calm voices and official phrases. Meanwhile, I was trying to understand how a man who kissed trophy bass had been reduced to paperwork. Life became a series of empty promises.

As the world kept moving forward, I was left trying to understand what forward even meant.

It did not take long before more details began to surface. Details I never asked for but could not avoid. I learned that the driver was driving without a license. She called multiple people to help her, even though she didn't try to help my dad. That in the dark of night, they attempted to hide her vehicle in hopes of not being caught.

There are images that arrive without invitation and refuse to leave.

I tried not to picture it. I tried not to imagine him alone on the side of that road. I tried not to imagine the silence of the fields or the way the emergency lights must have looked against the dark sky when he was finally found. But the mind does not always cooperate with what the heart wants.

What I felt most in those early days was not only grief, but disbelief. Not just that he was gone, but that the manner of it all felt so careless, so preventable, so avoidable.

The word "pending" became one I grew to resent.

Pending investigation. Pending arrest. Pending charges.

As if justice were something that could be scheduled neatly on a calendar.

Hours passed without updates. Then days. Every time my phone rang, my heart would tighten, wondering if it was news. Every time it wasn't, I felt let down. We were told the process takes time. Evidence must be gathered. Statements must be verified. Procedures must be followed.

Time was the one thing I no longer understood.

It felt cruel that the world expected patience when my entire life had been altered in an instant.

I wanted accountability. I wanted someone to look me in the eyes and say this would not be minimized. That his life mattered enough to obtain justice.

Instead, I learned how slowly the system moves.

And in that waiting, anger began to settle beneath the surface. It did not erupt, it only simmered quietly, with nowhere to land.

The following days pressed even harder. My dad's name moved beyond our family and into the public.

His accident was on the local news. His photo appeared on television screens, social media feeds, and in articles in the newspaper. Words like “hit and run” and “investigation” were repeated by anchors who had never known him. They spoke about timelines and the suspect. They discussed evidence and pending charges.

They told the story of how he died. They did not tell the story of how he lived.

I would catch glimpses of the coverage without meaning to. A headline shared. A clip playing in the background somewhere. Strangers commenting with opinions. Each time it felt jarring. To me my dad was not a segment on the evening news. He was not just another case number waiting to be solved. He was not a developing story.

He was the man who bought fries for crows. The one who lingered on the phone and the one who never missed a birthday call, and yet, there he was, reduced to a headline.

But to those that knew him knew he was so much more.

At his celebration of life, the line stretched farther than I could see from the doorway. It wrapped around the building and spilled onto the sidewalks that lined the streets, coats pulled tight against the cold, hands tucked into pockets as people waited patiently for their turn to step inside. Someone mentioned that it stretched for blocks. I believed them. There were simply too many faces to count.

I stood near the entrance for a moment and watched them. Men he had worked with. Neighbors. Friends from seasons of his life I only knew pieces of. People I had never met but who carried stories about him as if they had known him forever. They came to say goodbye to a man who would pull over to help change a tire. A man that was a friend to all. A man that loved life.

I knew my dad was loved. But seeing it like that felt almost unreal. The line never seemed to thin. It just kept coming.

Inside, tables were covered with food. Trays of sandwiches, homemade pasta salads, and cookies filled every available space, reminding me of when we lost my mom years earlier. Paper plates balanced carefully in hands while stories were shared. Moments of laughter woven gently between tears as people spoke about his humor, his generosity, his way of living fully without apology.

I nodded when expected. I thanked them for coming. I listened carefully as story after story confirmed what I had always known about him.

I should have felt something. Instead, I felt numb.

I sat at a table where the white tablecloth draped neatly over the edges, its corners pressed flat as if someone had taken great care in making everything look perfect. Chairs scraped softly against the floor as people stood to hug one another and others quickly filled the empty seats. The room hummed with conversation, remembrance, and love.

A plate of food sat untouched in front of me.

It wasn't a decision. It was a disconnect. My body felt like it had shut down alongside my world. Hunger did not exist. Neither did tears.

I watched hands reach for food, watched mouths move in conversation, watched grief express itself outwardly in ways that made sense.

Inside, I felt still.

It was disorienting to stand in a room filled with hundreds of people who loved him and feel hollow inside my own body. The love in that space was undeniable and yet, I could not access it. I watched others cry openly while I remained composed, almost detached, as if I were observing someone else's loss rather than my own.

Grief did not feel the way I expected it to. It did not erupt or collapse me. It quieted me.

It felt like standing in the middle of something enormous and feeling nothing at all.

That evening, after the line finally disappeared and the chairs were folded and stacked, I went home.

The house felt different the moment I walked in. Not in a way someone else might notice, but in the subtle way sound carries when something essential is missing. I closed the door behind me and stood there for a moment, still in my coat, listening.

There was no television murmuring in the background. No footsteps moving from room to room. No sounds of cars making their way down the road.

Just stillness. That was the hardest part. Nothing in the house announced that he was gone. There were no physical signs that a life had ended. Only an absence that could not be touched but could be felt everywhere.

I walked into the kitchen and leaned against the counter, staring at nothing in particular. I picked up my phone without thinking. For a split second, I almost expected to see his name there. A missed call. A voicemail. Something.

There was nothing.

I set the phone down and let the silence settle around me.

Earlier that day, hundreds of people had stood in line to honor him. The room was full. The air had been heavy with stories, laughter, and love until now, in the quiet of my own home, it felt as though all of it had drained away.

This was the part no one sees. The part after the crowd leaves. After the food is packed away. After the headlines move on to the next story. The part where you are left alone with the reality that there is no one older to call anymore.

In the weeks that followed, people slowly stopped showing up so the house grew even quieter. The casseroles stopped arriving. The phone calls became less frequent. But I couldn't blame them. There are only so many versions of, "I'm sorry" someone can offer before life calls them back to their own responsibilities.

Their worlds resumed. Mine did not.

I was left standing still, trying to understand how to live in a world where both of my parents were gone.

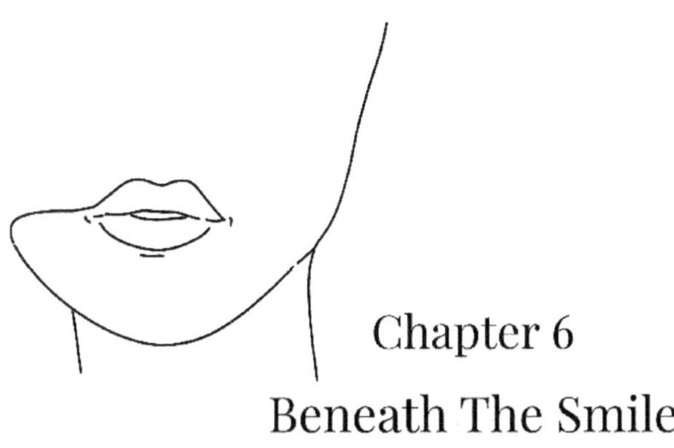

Chapter 6
Beneath The Smile

The silence left behind can be louder than any voice.

Chapter 6

Beneath The Smile

My birthday came ten days after my dad was killed.

For as long as I could remember, he had always been the first to call. No matter what was happening in his life his number on my phone would light up before anyone else's. It became something I expected, and something that I always looked forward to. It became something so steady that I stopped noticing how much I relied on it. It was never about the length of the conversation, it was about the consistency. The certainty. The quiet reassurance that I mattered to someone in a way that didn't fluctuate.

Even though I knew his phone number would never flash across the small screen of my phone again. I still found myself checking it, almost instinctively. I would glance down when it buzzed, just for a split second allowing myself to wonder. I waited for it in a way that didn't make sense, knowing full well that

"Dad" would never appear on my screen again, and yet, some part of me still hoped it would.

I held my phone a little longer that day. I checked it more times than I would admit. It is strange how grief works that way. Your mind understands what your heart resists. Even knowing he was gone, there was still a part of me that waited. Not because I believed he would call, but because I wasn't ready for him to stop.

The day moved forward the way birthdays always do. I answered text messages from friends and smiled when I was supposed to. We kept our tradition and went for taco pizza, sitting in the same booth, ordering the same thing, smiling at the same server. From the outside, it looked familiar. Predictable. Almost comforting, but I felt slightly removed from all of it.

The air felt heavier.

There were candles and conversations and the usual rhythm of celebration, yet underneath it all there was an absence that could not be disguised. When the pizza arrived, I tried to participate in the moment. I picked up a slice and took a bite. I chewed slowly. I swallowed because it felt expected. However, hunger did not exist the way it once had. The laughter around the table felt slightly out of sync with what was happening inside me. I moved the food around my plate more than I ate it, hoping no one would notice the difference.

Shortly after my birthday I returned to work. I told myself it was good to stay busy, that structure would help steady me, that being needed by someone else might quiet the noise inside my own head. The hospital where I worked felt familiar in a way that home no longer did. The steady rhythm of monitors and call lights created a kind of background hum that felt stabilizing. Patients depended on me. Families needed reassurance. It was easier to manage other people's pain than sit with my own. Grief did not interrupt what happened there. In those hallways, there was no room for collapse, so I leaned into that.

With the holidays approaching, I volunteered myself to work. I framed it as practical, even generous.

Someone had to cover Thanksgiving, and I was willing. But the truth was more layered than that. I did not want to sit at a table that felt incomplete. I did not want to face the empty space where my dad should have been or try to manufacture warmth that I did not feel. Working felt easier than explaining the heaviness I carried. It allowed me to avoid the quiet moments when absence becomes most obvious.

While my family gathered and traditions continued, I stayed at the hospital, moving from room to room, keeping myself in motion. It felt safer that way. There were patients who did not know my story and did not need to. They only needed care and I knew how to provide that.

Around the same time, my relationship with food shifted from something subtle to something structured. It began quietly after his celebration of life. I remember standing near the tables filled with casseroles and desserts while people shared stories and laughter, unable to bring myself to eat. Grief had taken up so much space that hunger felt irrelevant.

My body did not want nourishment. It wanted something steadier, something controllable.

But once my birthday and Thanksgiving had passed the restriction was no longer accidental. It was deliberate. Limiting. There was something almost soothing about the structure of it. It began to carry the same sense of order that my work schedule did. If I could not control court dates, investigations, or the finality of losing both of my parents, I could control what I allowed myself to consume or refuse.

It felt like the one area of my life where nothing was unpredictable.

At first, it felt disciplined rather than destructive. It felt like I was choosing something when so much had been chosen for me. But what I did not recognize then was how quickly discipline can turn into disappearance, and how quietly I was beginning to fade inside my own life.

Christmas arrived quietly, and if I'm honest, I don't remember much of it. I know there were presents under the tree, lights strung neatly on rooftops, and joyful music on the radio station. I know it happened, but I don't remember how it felt. Memory requires presence, and I was only partially there.

The one thing I will always remember is the kindness that surrounded us.

That year, the county police department quietly "adopted" our family for Christmas. They reached out and asked for the kid's Christmas lists, and somehow every item written down ended up beneath our tree. Gifts had been delivered with care by police officers who may not have known us personally but understood the weight of what we just lost.

I am not sure those officers realize just how much their generosity meant. In the middle of grief that had narrowed my world, they reminded me that compassion still existed outside of it.

By February, people had stopped whispering and started watching. They asked if I was sleeping. If I was eating. If I was okay. I answered the same way every time.

"I'm fine."

And when they pressed, I pushed back harder.

As winter continued to move forward towards spring, the absence of hunger stopped feeling accidental. It began to feel intentional. Shaped by my own self. It was subtle at first, almost invisible. But it was mine. By the time snow melted and leaned toward spring, I was exhausted from performing steadiness.

The world had adjusted to its new normal and life continued to move forward around me, and while everyone else resumed their rhythm, I quietly began creating one of my own.

One built on discipline, restraint, and on control.

I did not recognize it as disappearing. I only knew it felt steadier than the silence.

Chapter 7

400 Calories

Control can feel like survival when everything else feels lost.

Chapter 7

400 Calories

Just as the presence of others faded, so did my appetite. At first it felt small. Likely unnoticeable to others. I would find myself skipping breakfast because I wasn't hungry or having a smaller portion at dinner because nothing sounded good, but soon it became something else entirely. What began as absence soon evolved into intention.

There was something steady about saying no. About choosing not to eat. It started out quietly as I began paying attention to numbers. Calories became measurable in a way grief was not. I could count them. Reduce them. Control them. The hollow ache in my stomach became proof that I was succeeding at something. It became my new focus.

Four hundred calories a day became my rule.

Chicken broth. Oyster crackers. Water.

If I felt like I had miscalculated or allowed too much, I compensated. A longer workout or extra crunches before bed. An added set of stairs when the elevator was an option. When the holidays approached and eating felt unavoidable, I found other ways to maintain the illusion of control. Laxatives followed. I told myself it was discipline. That I was simply being careful. That strength looked like restraint.

Crying became harder, not because I was healing, but because I no longer had the physical energy to sustain it. My thoughts slowed and my responses grew muted. The sharp edges of grief felt less jagged, not because they had softened, but because I no longer had the strength to feel them fully. What settled in their place felt almost like peace.

But it wasn't peace, it was depletion.

Numbness settled over me like a thin blanket, light enough that I could still function, but heavy enough that I did not have to confront the full force of what I had lost. I mistook the absence of feeling for healing.

I picked up more hours at work, pouring what little energy I had into caring for others. It felt easier to focus on the patient's needs and charting than to acknowledge the quiet unraveling happening beneath the surface within me. There was comfort in the responsibility.

The more people in my personal life questioned me, the further I retreated. Concern felt intrusive. Offers of help felt threatening. When comments were spoken, I brushed them off. I told everyone I was fine. I told myself I was fine.

Somewhere beneath the surface, I understood my body was weakening. My clothes fit differently. My energy thinned. Climbing stairs left me winded, even though I would take them because I knew it burned more calories. My heart would race inside my chest. But a part of me did not resist it. There was something almost comforting about the way I felt. All of it evidence that I was shrinking something that was once too big to contain.

There was a quiet logic in my mind. If I became smaller, quieter, less demanding, perhaps the ache would disappear too. If there was less of me, maybe grief would become less too.

In my lowest moments, I imagined being reunited with my mom and dad. That thought brought a comfort I am not proud to admit. Even though I had children who needed me and a family who loved me, my rational thinking had dulled. Grief had reduced my world to a single question that looped relentlessly.

Why me?

That question echoed in the quiet spaces of my day. It followed me to work and lingered during charting. It sat beside me at night while I would lay awake in the dark. It filled the silence I had once tried to outrun.

I began to believe life might be easier without me in it. I never acted on those thoughts, but I also didn't fight them the way I should have either. I assumed my body would eventually give out, and part of me accepted that possibility.

Thankfully, there were two women who refused to let that happen.

My physician and my counselor had been meeting with me weekly since my dad died. They had watched the numbers change. They had listened to the exhaustion in my voice. They saw what I was unwilling to acknowledge. They became my safe place and the ones I could confide in. They asked harder questions than anyone else did, and they did not accept easy answers. They did not allow me to hide behind competence and composure.

What I did not know was that they spoke to one another when I was not in the room. They made calls I did not know were being made. They began building a plan while I continued believing I had everything under control.

Somewhere in the middle of that season, when everything inside me felt like it was unraveling, I made another decision that I thought would help my healing. I found a local chocolate labrador breeder and picked out a puppy.

I told myself it was therapy. That the companionship would help. But if I'm being honest, I was trying to recreate something I had lost. My dad had always had Hank. Where he was, Hank was close behind. There was comfort in that loyalty.

So, a few days later, I brought home the puppy and named him Harley—after my dad's motorcycle and the freedom that he loved, and the parts of him I wasn't ready to let go of. I held that puppy close and convinced myself that this was healing. I believed caring for him would anchor me, that love in any form would be enough. And for a while, it felt like it might.

But grief doesn't negotiate that way, and neither does self-destruction.

At one follow-up appointment, my nurse practitioner sat across from me with a steadiness that felt different than before. There was no frustration in her voice and no attempt to soften the truth.

“Abbey,” she said gently, “I can’t do this alone anymore. You need more help than I can give you right now. I cannot sit back and watch you die. I’ve made arrangements for you to get the help you need. Would you like to call your family, or would you like me to?”

The words landed without resistance.

For the first time in months, I did not argue. I did not defend myself. I did not insist that I was fine.

I let her make the call.

Chapter 8

The Double Doors

Sometimes saving your life begins with surrender.

Chapter 8

The Double Doors

A grueling four months after my dad was killed and on the exact day the girl responsible for taking his life was finally arrested, I walked through the double set of doors at the University of Iowa Hospital and gave back all control in order to save my own.

The doors opened automatically. I did not. My body moved forward, but my pride stayed behind. I did not walk in healed. I walked in willing, because I knew if I didn't choose this, eventually the choice would no longer be mine.

The timing did not feel poetic. It felt almost cruel. Accountability had finally arrived for him, and yet in the same breath, I had to admit I was losing myself. Justice and surrender existed within the same few hours, and I remember thinking how strange it was that both could feel heavy in such different ways.

The initial exam left little room for denial. My bloodwork confirmed what I had refused to acknowledge. I was malnourished. My electrolytes were dangerously low. The EKG revealed abnormalities suggesting my heart was either on the verge of a heart attack or had already endured more strain than it should have. My body had been compensating quietly for months.

My heart had been working overtime to keep me alive.

It felt symbolic in a way that was almost too obvious. My heart had emotionally shattered months earlier, and now it was physically struggling to hold on. But unlike my dad, I was being given another chance at life.

Only this time it was up to me to choose it.

For the next three months, I ate when I was told to eat. I slept when I was told to sleep. I woke up on their schedule, not mine. My autonomy was exchanged for structure. My freedom was replaced with routine. I handed over my entire self to strangers at the lowest point of my life.

For someone who had tried so desperately to control everything, surrender felt foreign.

And strangely relieving.

There was something steady about the predictability. Meals arrived whether I wanted them or not. I did not have to debate with myself or calculate calories. Dinner plates were placed in front of us with food we were not allowed to turn away. No crumbs could be left behind. Bedtime snacks of Pop-Tarts and chocolate milk filled our stomachs before lights were turned off on schedule as the 1JPW techs made their nightly rounds.

Mornings began the same way each day. Vitals were taken. Bloodwork was drawn. Medication was administered. All before meeting the other patients at the scale for weigh-ins while wearing our paper-thin gowns. Vulnerability at its highest.

And yet, inside that rigid structure, I felt something unexpected.

Safety.

I did not have to decide anything. I did not have to defend my grief or explain my anger. I did not have to convince anyone I was fine. For the first time since my dad died, I was not responsible for holding myself together.

It is hard to admit, but that sterile hospital environment became the safest place I had felt in months.

And yet, life did not completely pause.

Somehow, in the middle of structured meals and therapy sessions, I continued my nursing classes online. I logged in from a small desk inside a place that had just declared my body unsafe. I studied medications and nutrition and while learning about myself in ways no textbook could teach. It felt almost surreal. I was working toward a profession built on caring for others while being forced to finally care for myself.

There was something grounding about it. A quiet reminder that I still had a future, that I was not just a diagnosis. I was still me. Still capable and still moving forward, even if it looked different than I had imagined.

Visitors were allowed during certain hours. Not everyone could come, and not everyone did. But the ones who showed up meant more than they probably realized. They sat in uncomfortable wooden chairs and tried to act normal. They asked about my classes. They told me small pieces of outside life. Ordinary details that felt extraordinary in that space.

For the family and friends that couldn't show up in person, most showed up in other ways. Handwritten notes arrived folded carefully into envelopes. Some included photos, while others included verses or inspirational quotes. Some sent just a few sentences and a signature at the bottom of the inside of store-bought cards. I understood that words are hard to find in seasons like that. Sometimes "thinking of you" is all a person can manage.

Each piece was laid neatly on the small table beside my bed. I read them more than once, and on harder days, I often read them again.

Their presence, whether in a chair across from me or in ink on paper, felt steady. It reminded me that this place was temporary. That there was still a life waiting for me outside those doors.

But safety did not only come from the outside.

Inside those walls, I began to realize I was surrounded by people who were not there to control me, but to protect me.

The doctors did not feel like authority figures dictating my life. They felt like advocates instead of someone there to place blame. They challenged me, but they stood beside me while I did the work. For the first time in months, I did not feel like I was fighting alone.

They were not trying to silence my grief, they were trying to help me survive it.

That distinction mattered more than I can explain.

Inpatient treatment was not gentle work. My therapists asked hard questions I could no longer avoid. I cried in ways I hadn't allowed myself to in years. I felt the anger that I was trying to avoid. I found myself angry with the driver, the justice system, God, and at myself. I broke down. I unpacked memories I had sealed shut.

And somewhere in the middle of that unhinged unloading, I started to feel something I hadn't felt in a long time. I began to feel more human.

In the quiet hours between therapy sessions, I began to see something clearly. I had never fully grieved my mom. At eleven, I learned how to survive by staying composed. I learned to absorb pain without speaking it. Losing my dad did not just fracture my present, it reopened my past.

When my mom died, I learned to tighten and perform. When my dad died, I tried to control and disappear. But inside those hospital walls, I was allowed to be undone without being abandoned.

That realization alone began to stitch something back together. I was beginning to feel like I belonged.

There was a strange closeness that formed quickly among the patients. When someone new arrives they are taken in quickly. In a matter of days, we knew pieces of one another that others in our lives never had. Pain does that, it removes small talk. It goes straight to the truth. We leaned on one another in ways that felt raw but real.

There were hard days. However, strangely enough there was laughter, too.

An environment that looked clinical and controlled from the outside felt unexpectedly unguarded inside. It was safe and it was honest. Honesty was something I had been avoiding for years, and safety was something I had not felt since I was a child.

Our days were structured in ways that left little room for hiding. Group therapy filled the mornings, chairs arranged in a circle where there was nowhere to look except at one another. We spoke about things most people avoid at dinner tables. All of our fears, shame, grief, and secrets would come out. There was no small talk. There was no pretending. Just honesty.

Physical therapy took us to the hospital's swimming pool, where the weight of our bodies felt lighter in the water than they did on land. I remember the quiet echo of splashes against tile and the strange comfort of movement without pressure. When the weather softened and spring began to return, they brought us outside. We stretched in the sunlight. We played simple games. The warmth on my skin felt unfamiliar at first, like I had been indoors for far too long, not just physically, but emotionally.

Music therapy surprised me the most. We sat in a dim room and listened to songs that resonated with us. We spoke about lyrics that felt like they had been written for our own stories. Sometimes we meditated. Sometimes we cried. Sometimes we just closed our eyes and allowed ourselves to feel without fixing anything. It was a sense of comfort as our therapist would speak over us in such a loving manner, reminding me of what it would be like to have a mother.

Occupational therapy gently pushed us back toward normal life. We practiced grocery shopping, learning how to walk through aisles without fear. We cooked simple meals together. Once, we even went out to a restaurant. Sitting in a booth with a menu in my hands felt empowering. Something so ordinary had once held so much control over me. Now it was becoming neutral again.

None of it was dramatic, but all of it was healing.

Each session, each routine, each small exposure reminded me that living did not have to feel like a battle. It could feel structured and supported. Most of all, it was beginning to feel possible.

When I first walked through those double doors, I believed I had failed. I believed surrender meant weakness. I believed asking for help meant I had lost.

By the time I walked back out, I understood something different. Surrender was not giving up, it was choosing to live.

For the first time in months, I was not trying to disappear. I was choosing to stay.

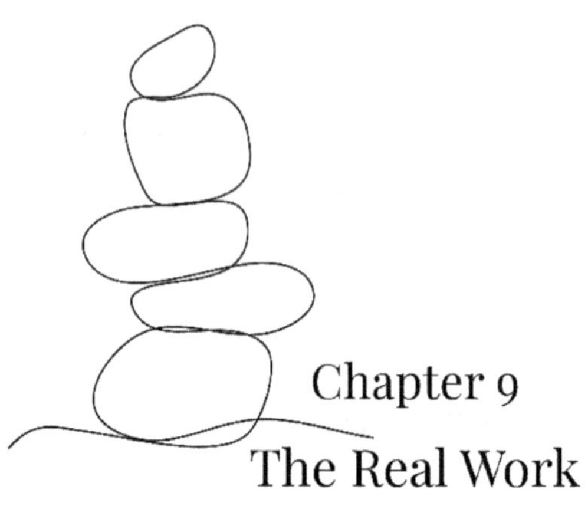

Chapter 9
The Real Work

Healing begins the moment we allow life to move forward again.

Chapter 9

The Real Work

After being discharged from the hospital, the real work began.

There were no more locked doors. No more scheduled meals. No nurses checking in at the top of every hour. The safety I had found inside those walls did not disappear, but it no longer surrounded me.

Healing was no longer contained within a unit. It had to travel with me.

I transitioned into the University of Iowa's partial hospitalization program for six more weeks. It was a bridge between being watched over and standing on my own. Five days a week I returned to the hospital for intensive therapy. There I sat in unfamiliar rooms with the same familiar therapists and patients that were discharged before me. All who had carried me through inpatient. The familiarity helped. It felt less like being released and more like being gradually untethered. At night, instead of returning to a hospital bed, I returned to a hotel room with one of my closest friends I made along this journey. We no longer had techs in the hallway checking in on us or a structured time that lights needed to be out. There were no trays to finish or vitals to record.

Just quiet.

Just her and I.

We would sit cross-legged on the stiff hotel comforters talking about everything and nothing at the same time. Sometimes we processed the day. Sometimes we laughed about things only people who have been in a locked unit together could understand. There is a strange bond that forms when you meet someone at your lowest. It strips away small talk. It removes pretense.

We would often go outside of the hotel to take a walk for fresh air or join in on the college town experiences. Some nights we celebrated finishing a full meal without fear, knowing the next morning we would once again be weighed in. We watched mindless television. We talked about what life might look like when we were both fully back in it.

Healing did not always look heavy. Sometimes it looked like two girls in a hotel room, choosing to stay.

On the weekends, I went home.

That was the real test.

Home looked the same as it always had. My children were there. My responsibilities were waiting. The world had not paused for my healing. It had simply been waiting for me to reenter it.

The program was designed to ease the transition from safety to uncertainty. From structure to choice. From being told what to eat, when to sleep, when to speak, to deciding those things for myself again.

And that was the part that scared me. Inside the hospital, surrender had saved me. Outside of it, I had to choose to stay saved.

I returned to work. I logged back into my nursing classes. I continued with outpatient therapy five days a week until I officially transitioned out of it. I tried to merge the girl who had surrendered with the woman who still had responsibilities waiting for her.

Life did not slow down to accommodate my healing. It simply resumed.

That summer, we went back to Lake Kabetogama.

The same lake where my dad had risen before sunrise to cast his pole into the glass like water. The same dock where I once sat swinging my legs into the water under the same quiet stretch of northern Minnesota sky that had always felt like a second home.

This time, we carried him with us.

We loaded the boat the way we always had. Life jackets. Snacks. Quiet conversation. But tucked carefully among us was the small container that held what remained of him and Hank.

We rode out toward Jug Island, his favorite place. The water was calm that morning. Too calm. As if even the lake knew to be gentle. I remember the stillness. The way we all stood a little closer than usual. The way grief felt different there.

We let him go where he had always felt most alive.

The ashes hit the water and disappeared quickly, folding into the surface without resistance. No splash. No dramatic moment, just a quiet return.

For the first time since he died, something inside me softened.

He wasn't in a courtroom. He wasn't in police reports. He wasn't in headlines or case numbers. He was in the water underneath the flawless sky. He was in the quiet ripple of the waves as they slowly brushed against the rocks. And somehow, that felt right.

When we came home, life was waiting.

Grief does not pause your life or responsibilities. It simply weaves itself through them.

Somewhere in that season, my marriage quietly unraveled. We were young. Grief changes people.

Survival changes people. And sometimes growth reveals fractures that were already there.

I did not fail at staying alive, but I could not force something to remain whole that no longer was. We proceeded with a divorce while maintaining what would be best for our two young children.

And then, just six months after she was sentenced to ten years in prison, the girl who killed my dad was released. The system that had already felt hollow now felt cruel.

I had fought to stay alive and she was free.

Grief did not end with discharge. It stretched into ordinary days. It appeared in quiet moments. Within anniversaries and milestones. And it seemed the heaviest in silence.

I mourned my dad, and I mourned my mom all over again.

This is where I began making a conscious decision for myself.

I no longer wanted to live in the quiet fog of countless medications. They had steadied me when I needed stabilizing, and I am grateful for that season. But somewhere along the way, steady had started to feel numb, and numb was no longer enough. I didn't want to simply survive my life. I wanted to feel it.

Even if feeling meant pain, anger, or tears that had nowhere to fall.

I was tired of cycling through the same internal question, *why me?* It had become a reflex. Every hardship, setback, or reminder of loss seemed to circle back to that same thought, and I could feel myself spiraling inside it.

So I started researching.

I found a therapist who specialized in Cognitive Behavioral Therapy, a form of therapy built not on silencing thoughts, but examining them. Challenging them. Replacing distorted narratives with ones rooted in truth instead of fear.

For the first time, I wasn't just asking someone to help me cope. I was asking someone to help me grow.

CBT required something different from me. It required participation and honesty. It required me to sit with thoughts I had long accepted as facts and ask if these thoughts were actually true.

Was life happening *to* me? Or was I still capable of shaping how I responded to it?

That question changed everything because slowly, the pattern of “why me?” began to shift.

Not overnight but gradually. I began replacing it with something quieter. Something steadier.

What now? What can I learn? What is still within my control?

It was not about denying what had happened. It was about refusing to let it define what came next. For the first time, the control I had been chasing through restriction and avoidance began to look different. It looked like choosing to feel.

Somewhere in the middle of rebuilding, a friend from my CNA class insisted I go on a blind date with her brother. I almost didn’t. It felt too soon for something new. Too fragile. Too uncertain. I wasn't sure if there was room in my heart or life that I was trying hard to reestablish.

But I went.

Not because I was ready, but because I was willing.

That night wasn't dramatic, but it provided a sense of ease I hadn't felt in a long time. He didn't try to fix me. He didn't shy away from me because of the weight of my story. We sat in silence when silence was needed and he had a way of making the air lighter when conversations became heavy.

It wasn't that my grief disappeared. It was that it didn't feel like it made me too much.

For the first time in a long time, I felt steady in someone else's presence.

Chapter 10

Blended

Some lives don't merge all at once. They learn their rhythm slowly.

Chapter 10

Blended

That steadiness did not mean life suddenly became simple.

Falling in love is one thing. That was the easy part. Love feels instinctive and doesn't require extra work. It moves quickly and confidently. Compromises come easily. It's unburdened by logistics or negotiations. What we felt was immediate and certain in a way neither of us questioned.

Building a life together is something completely different.

It is where conversations grew heavier. Plans required coordination instead of spontaneous decisions without the worry of impact. We were two adults responsible for our own children, school schedules, holidays, financial obligations and emotional histories.

Blending two already moving worlds is something entirely different. It is where tough choices had to be made. Where boundaries are unclear even when you think you've drawn them out. Where loyalties existed long before you entered the picture. Where you are humbled in ways you never knew possible.

When we chose each other, we weren't just choosing romance. We were choosing history. Children. Schedules. Traditions already in motion. Emotional landscapes that had been forming for years.

Yet, beneath the complexity, the steadiness between us still continued to grow.

Our engagement wasn't elaborate, it was simple and intentional. It was quiet and uncomplicated, something we both desired. It felt certain. Then, a short five weeks later, we boarded a plane for the Gulf Coast of Florida and eloped. Not because we were running from anything, but because we knew what we were choosing.

It wasn't about anything other than commitment.

Just as the sun met the ocean without resistance, we stood before each other and said yes to something that would stretch us in ways we couldn't yet see.

And, just like that we became an instant family of seven.

There is something bold about the word *blended.* It sounds smooth and cohesive, naturally easy. In reality, it is trying and demanding. It often requires constant awareness and perspective, especially when emotions are high.

When we returned home, blended life began immediately. Schedules overlapped and holidays required negotiations. Traditions collided and expectations slowly had to be adjusted. While we enjoyed countless moments of laughter, joy, and beauty, we also shared moments that felt heavy and fragile.

There was a night not long after we married when everything inside me felt louder than I could manage. It wasn't about him, the children, or the life we were building. It was about the overwhelm that had nowhere to land. Grief, responsibility, adjustment, exhaustion, everything that was building up that I had convinced myself I was handling well.

That night, I didn't.

In a moment of emotional overload, I responded in a way that startled me. It was private and brief, but it revealed something I could no longer ignore. Even in a season filled with love and hope, I still did not have the tools to sit with certain kinds of discomfort. I had learned how to survive devastation. I had learned how to function through chaos. But I had not fully learned how to regulate stress when it arrived in quieter forms.

The physical reminder would fade. The lesson would not.

It became clear to me that healing was not just about surviving what had happened. It was about learning how to live well afterward. I did not want to move through life reacting to overwhelm. I wanted to understand it. I wanted to build something steadier inside myself.

That realization led me to once again seek out a therapist. I wanted more than coping. I wanted the tools needed to challenge the patterns that surfaced when I felt stretched too thin. I wanted to learn how to feel without unraveling.

For the first time, I was not just trying to endure my life. I was choosing to engage with it differently.

Our life was layered. It was complicated, beautiful and exhausting all in the same breath. It required kindness on the days you didn't feel like offering it. It required restraint when your emotions are louder than your wisdom. It required humility when you realize love does not erase past wounds.

We were not walking into something polished and predictable. We were learning, in real time, how to merge two histories into one future. There was no handbook for that. No direction for navigating loyalty, discipline, tenderness, and fairness all at once.

There were seasons that stretched us in ways we did not anticipate. They revealed us and also those around us. They softened us in ways we didn't know we needed softening. Seasons where loyalties felt tangled and where I felt like I was living a life that was not fully mine. A life shared in ways I had never imagined for myself.

And yet, it felt right. Not easy or effortless. But right.

I would be lying if I didn't say mistakes were made along the way. I made mistakes, and he did too, but like with any mistake a lesson is learned.

Some lessons we learned quietly, after hard conversations behind closed doors. Some we learned from each other through trial and humility. And some, unexpectedly, we learned from the kids themselves.

I loved our children fiercely, even on the days I felt invisible or misunderstood. Even on those days I wondered if I was doing any of it well. Loving them was never the difficult part, the uncertainty was.

There were nights when the house finally grew quiet, when the lights were off, doors were closed and they were all safely tucked away in their beds, that I would sit alone in my thoughts. Or after the busy weekend, when they returned to their other homes and the silence would suddenly feel heavier. It was in those times that I wondered if they ever felt invisible or misunderstood too. Whether the shifting of houses and schedules ever made them question where they belonged.

Blended life required more patience than I naturally possessed and more forgiveness than I felt equipped to give. It exposed my insecurities and forced me to confront the parts of myself that still wanted control.

But it also deepened my capacity for love.

There is a quiet strength required in choosing a life that doesn't look like the one you once imagined. A maturity that comes from saying, this may not have been the original plan, but it is the path.

The path we were determined to pave and the future my husband and I worked so hard to build.

Through blended family life. Through infertility and waiting. Through hope that didn't always come on our timeline.

And then pregnancy.

I gave birth to our baby boy just ten days before graduating nursing school. I walked across that stage exhausted and overwhelmed but fiercely proud. It felt symbolic in a way I didn't yet have words for. Years earlier, I had doubted whether I would survive my grief. Now I was holding new life and completing something I had once feared I could not finish.

Shortly eight months later, another pregnancy. Another baby boy. And just like that, our family became nine.

Nine.

Nine still sounds expansive when I say it.

It was loud. It was messy. It was not easy. But it was beautiful.

And it was ours.

And, if I had to do it all over again, knowing the hard years, the strained conversations, the growing pains, I would still choose this life.

Because it shaped me. Because it deepened me. Because it forced me to become unfiltered.

Chapter 11
Becoming Unfiltered

Growth often happens quietly, long before anyone else notices.

Chapter 11

Becoming Unfiltered

Growth rarely announces itself. It does not arrive with applause or visible markers that signal you have crossed into something more. More often, it comes quietly. It happens somewhere between therapy appointments and job changes. Or between difficult conversations on long nights when neither of you quite knows how you're going to get through it, but somehow you do.

Blended life did not magically smooth itself out. Marriage did not become effortless simply because we loved one another. Healing did not become permanent. Pieces of us were continuously shifting, while old assumptions were challenged and patterns slowly unlearned.

There were seasons where we were both tired in different ways. Times where he carried burdens I could not fix, and I had to learn that loving someone does not mean rescuing them. There were times when I carried things he could not fully understand, no matter how much he wanted to.

We both had our own demons and we both had our own work to do. There are scars that remain and private battles that aren't my story to tell. Pieces of our lives that will forever remain within us. The part of us where maturing together meant recognizing where support ends and ownership begins.

Somewhere along the way, I stopped expecting marriage to save me. That was not its job. Its job was partnership. And partnership requires two people willing to stay in the room when things get uncomfortable.

There were hard conversations that repeated the same tender subjects more than once. Moments of tension that lingered longer than we both preferred. Times where I questioned whether loving deeply always meant facing these challenges head on, hoping to find the courage together.

So, therapy continued. Not because I was broken, but because I was building. I wanted to do more than survive, I wanted to thrive. I learned how to feel anger without self-destruction. How to communicate disappointment without retreat. How to listen without reacting. And how to recognize when old patterns were surfacing and making the choice to respond differently.

This time I wasn't shutting down. I wasn't disappearing or searching for an outlet of something I could control. I was speaking. For the first time in my life I wasn't trying to act like I was finc, I was going to fight for a way to thrive.

I didn't find my voice all at once. Between therapy sessions, I began to find it in ink. I started writing more intentionally. At first it was messy. Scribbles in the margins of journals, lists of things I could control, inspirational quotes to get me through hard times. I often wrote out questions that I may never get the answers to.

Additionally, it became a safe place to express anger in a healthy way. I wrote a letter to the girl that killed my dad as a form of release. Journaling became a place where I didn't have to filter my words or soften the truth. It was simply a place that held it.

For years I managed my feelings by controlling and staying composed for others. Writing was different. I was able to articulate what was hard and admit what I needed. I didn’t survive this life to continue to feel mediocre. The more honest I became with myself the more grounded I became in other areas of my life.

Becoming unfiltered did not mean becoming loud. It meant becoming honest. I made the choice to become honest with myself and honest with those around me. Instead of always doing and saying what others wanted to hear, I asked myself what would be best for me.

I realized that there is strength in surviving tragedy. But there is a different kind of strength in staying present when life is simply hard. Marriage is hard, but we stayed. Raising children is hard, but you don’t give up. Diagnoses are hard, but you continue to put one foot in front of the other.

I stopped asking, “Why me?”

As the noise inside me softened, I finally heard it.

That quiet steadiness began shaping more than my private life. It began shaping my voice.

What started as journaling slowly moved beyond the pages. Invitations came to speak. I stood in large rooms at women's conferences and in small basements of churches. I did not feel qualified in the way I once believed speakers had to be. I did not have everything in life figured out. But I had lived it and I had my story to tell. That felt like enough and gave me the courage.

Standing in front of others and telling the truth about grief, control, losing both of my parents and nearly losing myself, felt different than I expected. It did not reopen wounds. It revealed how much they had healed. The shame that once kept me quiet had loosened its grip. The parts of my story that once felt fragile now felt purposeful.

I was no longer speaking from the center of my pain. I was speaking from the other side of it.

There is something steady about naming your survival out loud. It reminds you that you are not who you were in the darkest chapters. It reminds you that growth is real, and your pages are worth turning.

At home, that same steadiness had settled in. Our marriage was not always perfect, but it was grounded. We had weathered enough tension to know that discomfort did not signal collapse. We had learned how to listen without defensiveness and how to apologize without pride swallowing the words. Our children continued to grow older alongside us which reminded us that we are all living this life for the first time. There was a maturity in us that had not been there before.

My mental health was no longer a fragile thing I tiptoed around. It was something I actively tended and spoke of. Therapy was no longer crisis management but maintenance. I paid attention to sleep and prioritized my physical health as well. I honored boundaries and noticed when stress tried to rise. I met it with tools instead of avoidance.

I was beginning to figure out how to live life with less worry.

Faith, too, had shifted from something I reached for in desperation to something woven into the ordinary. I no longer searched for dramatic signs to prove God was present. I began noticing the smaller blessings around me.

I began newfound friendships that were rooted in faith. Conversations felt less surface-level and more anchoring. I saw glimpses of God in my children's eyes. I would find rocks, spilled milk, and scraps of paper, all in the shape of hearts. Reminding me, I am constantly surrounded by His presence.

Sunsets became something I felt instead of simply admired. As the sun lowered itself into the horizon, melting quietly into the edge of the earth, I felt the same surrender settle inside me. The day would end whether I was ready or not, and yet there was comfort in its rhythm.

The silence I heard when crying out alone opened my ears to His true gifts I have received. My kids' laughter, the crows calling from the trees, the light rain on the roof on the days I needed peace so badly. For years the thoughts in my head had always been too loud to notice the blessings that surrounded me. When the internal noise quieted, I could finally hear them.

By this point in my life, I believed I had faced the hardest battles I would ever know. I had lost both of my parents. I had confronted my own self-destruction. I had rebuilt my health, my voice, and my faith. My husband and I began to feel more steady in blended family life. I felt anchored in ways I once thought were impossible.

When you begin to feel anchored, it does not mean the storms have passed. It means you have learned how to stand when they arrive.

Anxiety did not disappear from my life. It simply changed shape. It no longer dictated my decisions or convinced me I was on the verge of collapse. It showed up in smaller ways. In moments of overthinking and in ways in which worst-case scenarios still flickered through my mind. But now I had the tools and awareness. I knew the difference between a passing wave and a rising tide.

The difference was not the absence of fear. It was the absence of panic.

I no longer felt consumed by my own thoughts. I could notice them without becoming them. I could feel uneasy without assuming it meant disaster. That did not make me immune to anxiety, but it made me less controlled by it.

And because I had learned to live without constant bracing, I believed that I was prepared for whatever life placed in front of me.

I did not yet understand that life does not wait for you to feel ready before presenting the next challenge. Only this time it was not a test of my heart, but of my body.

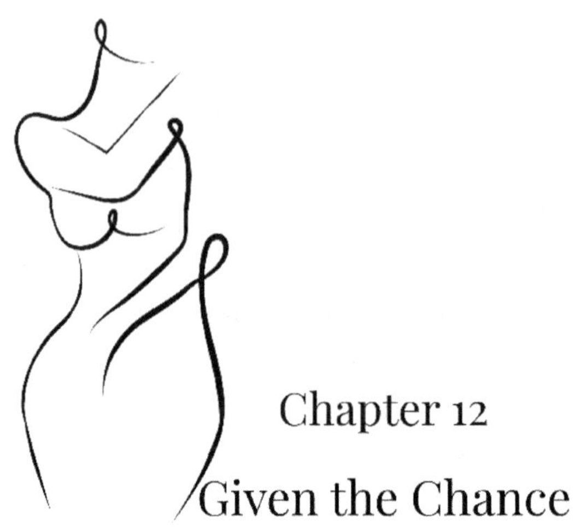

Chapter 12
Given the Chance

Choosing yourself can be one of the bravest decisions you make.

Chapter 12

Given the Chance

For years, I have lived with an awareness that my body carries more than just my own story.

Long before surgery was ever part of the conversation, there were lumpectomies. Two of them, both nearly two decades ago. Each time introducing a brief season of waiting before the word benign allowed life to resume its rhythm. At the time, I was young enough to believe that reassurance meant resolution. I returned back to life while raising children, finishing school, and building a life that felt full and forward moving.

But over the last five years, the watching intensified. Mammograms that led to ultrasounds. Ultrasounds that led to MRIs. The phrase “routine surveillance" became familiar, though it never quite brought comfort. Each appointment carried a quiet tension that lingered longer than the healthcare providers could see. I would sit in white sterile exam rooms pretending I wasn't counting years in my head.

Thirty-nine.

The age my mom was when cancer took her has never felt like just a number. It has lived quietly in the background of birthdays and milestones, growing louder as I approached it, and a sense of relief when I surpassed it myself.

Then, a year ago, another routine MRI resulted in another biopsy.

It was not the first, but it was the one that shifted something in me. The waiting felt heavier. Not because the results were catastrophic, but because I was tired of living between scans. Tired of anxiety creeping back in, shortly after it had settled. Tired of bracing for a phone call that could divide my life into before and after.

For years, I had worked to steady my mind. Now I was being given options to protect my body.

This decision was not born out of panic.

It was born out of clarity.

Clarity that had been forming quietly over years of appointments and waiting rooms. It came from understanding my family history may not be an immediate threat but can be used as useful information. I told myself I did not want to continue living in surveillance mode, measuring my life in six-month increments between scans.

I had grown accustomed to the rhythm of monitoring. The phone calls asking me to return for additional imaging and offering polite reassurance in a careful tone providers use when they are trying to remain neutral. Each time, I told myself I could handle it. And I am sure I could, but handling something and wanting to live inside it are not the same thing.

The biopsy results a year ago were not with urgent worry. It did not come with additional testing or treatment. But it came with enough uncertainty to shift my posture. Enough to make me sit longer with the question I had quietly avoided.

What if I continued to wait? What if I continued to watch and wonder?

I had spent too much of my earlier life reacting to loss and tragedy. Overcome with outcomes I never desired. This time, I had the opportunity to choose before something chose me.

The conversations with my doctors were thorough and measured. We discussed risk percentages and genetics. We talked in detail about surgery outcomes and expectations. We weighed options about expanders, implants, recovery, and reconstruction. I asked questions I never imagined I would be asking. I took notes. I went home and read more. I prayed for guidance rather than escape.

At night, when the house was quiet and my children were asleep, I would sit with the weight of all of it. Not in fear, but in reflection. I would think about my mom at thirty-nine. I would think about my own children growing older. I would think about how fiercely I had fought to stay alive years earlier when grief tried to take me under.

I did not survive all of that to sit passively in possibility.

Choosing surgery was not about assuming the worst. It was about honoring the life I have now. It was about recognizing that courage sometimes looks less like endurance and more like prevention.

For years, control meant shrinking myself. Now, it meant protecting myself. And once that realization settled in, the decision felt easier.

The morning of surgery did not feel heavy, it felt intentional.

I had already done the emotional work long before I even stepped into the hospital. I had researched and sat in consultation rooms with information spread out before me. I had cried in quiet moments when the decision pressed against my chest and I had prayed for clarity as I went to bed each night. By the time the morning of surgery arrived, I was not searching for certainty, I was walking toward it.

As I changed into the hospital gown, I caught myself taking in the current state of my own image. I wasn't just preparing for surgery. I was saying goodbye to a version of my body that had carried me through adolescence, pregnancy, nursing babies, and through every season of becoming a woman. There is a complicated grief that comes with removing something that is a part of who you are, but also a part that could change your life in an instant. It is both preventive and permanent. I told myself it was empowering, but I was still feeling deeply emotional.

When I woke up after surgery, the pain was immediate and undeniable. My chest felt tight. I was wrapped and compressed. The expanders beneath my skin were creating a pressure that was impossible to ignore. Tubes and drains reminded me that healing is rarely graceful. Recovery required a humility I had not anticipated. It was humbling. I needed help sitting up and showering. I had to ask my husband, and those closest to me, for help performing simple tasks that once felt automatic. For someone who has always prided herself on stubborn independence, the vulnerability stretched me in unexpected ways. The love I had for my husband grew exponentially.

In the days after surgery, my independence had to loosen.

It was often not just family who stepped into the quiet, practical spaces of recovery, even though thankfully I had a few that did. Others checked in through text messages, reminding me to ask if I needed anything, and I appreciated the sentiment. But the ones who showed up physically, who walked through the door carrying meals, helped adjust pillows, and who sat beside me while I moved slowly from room to room, were friends.

Women who had no obligation to be there beyond love.

There was a time in my life when I would have insisted that I could manage alone. I would have minimized the pain, declined the help, and protected the illusion of strength. This time, I let them stay. I let them see the drains, the exhaustion, and the part of me that I would normally hide. I let them witness the unfiltered version of healing.

And instead of feeling exposed, I felt supported.

It was a quiet reminder that family is sometimes defined less by title and more by presence.

The first few weeks were the hardest emotionally. I had prepared for physical discomfort, but I had not fully prepared for the shock of seeing my body altered so dramatically. The swelling and suture lines left an unfamiliar shape staring back at me in the mirror. I was grateful and grieving at the same time. Grateful that I had the option to act before a diagnosis forced my hand. Grieving the loss of what had once felt natural and known.

There were plenty of days I avoided mirrors altogether. Then there were other days when I stood in front of one longer than I meant to. Staring at the figure in front of me, trying to reconcile strength with loss. Body image became louder than I expected during those early weeks. I knew I had been given the choice, and for me it was the right decision. I still had to process the change.

But this time, I did not turn against my body.

That is the difference.

Years ago, when grief consumed me, I tried to make myself smaller. I believed control meant restriction, disappearance, erasing myself in quiet ways that felt powerful at the time. Now, control meant advocacy. It meant protecting the life I had fought so hard to rebuild. It meant enduring temporary discomfort for long-term peace.

The reconstruction process is not finished. I am sitting here, an aging Harley by my side, still in it. Expanders remain for now, stretching skin that once felt effortless, reminding me daily that healing is ongoing. In a few short months, another surgery will remove them and they will be replaced with implants. I will have another recovery and another period of surrender. This chapter of my life is still being written.

Recovery has been grueling at times. It has required patience that did not come easy and rest that I often resisted. Anxiety has visited, especially while waiting for the pathology reports to come in or in the quiet moments before follow-up appointments, but it no longer consumes me the way it once did. I recognize it and am able to breathe through it. I remind myself that preparedness is not panic.

This decision was not light, and it was not out of fear. It was born out of clarity and taking back control.

My mom did not get the opportunity to choose prevention. She did not get decades of imaging, genetic discussions, treatment plans, or surgical consultations laid out before her. Cancer already decided that for her.

But I was given a choice.

I chose this for myself, because I finally understand that my life is worth protecting. I chose this for my children, because I want to be present for more than the big milestones. I want to watch them blow out candles year after year, sit in crowded auditoriums waiting for their names to be called, and witness them step into adulthood knowing that their mom is still in the stands. I want to see them become parents one day in a way that my own mom never had the chance to witness in me. And I chose this for my husband, who has stood beside me through every pit and peak of our own story. Through the versions of me that were steady and the ones that needed the support. Knowing it is our love that is the foundation of this family, and I intend to protect the life we have worked so hard to build.

Most of all, I chose to stay.

My mom didn't get the chance, but I did.

Chapter 13

The Story Continues

Every life holds a story still unfolding.

Chapter 13

The Story Continues

I used to believe the story ended at the hardest chapter.

That loss would define it. That grief would shape its tone. That survival would be the climax, and everything afterward would feel like an epilogue.

I know better now.

The story does not have to end with devastation. It continues in the quiet choices that follow. It can restart in the mornings when you wake up and decide to participate. And it's found in the little moments you notice that once would have passed you by.

I no longer wait for life to prove itself to me. I meet it where it stands.

I show up for the ordinary days because I understand now that ordinary is a miracle in itself. I lean into the noise of my home. Most days it's loud, but the rhythm of the laughter and late-night conversations that once felt guaranteed, now keep me in the moment. I feed the crows without sadness, only remembrance. I watch the sunset lower into the horizon, and I stay long enough to see it disappear completely, trusting that darkness has never once prevented morning.

This is no longer about survival. This is about living.

I used to ask for signs that everything would be okay, now I recognize that I am living inside the answer.

Somewhere along the way, I stopped hiding my story.

Not because it became easier to tell, but because I realized it was not meant to stay contained. The same voice that once whispered, "why me?" now finds itself standing in rooms full of people who are carrying their own invisible chapters.

When I speak, I do not speak as someone who has life completely figured out. I speak as someone who has learned that pain does not mean failure. I speak to show that mental health is not weakness, and that asking for help is not surrender, but strength.

I see myself in the eyes of some of the women who linger afterwards. The ones who say, "I thought I was the only one." I know that sentence. I have felt it too. And every time I hear it, I am reminded that stories do not heal in isolation. Some of my favorite messages I receive are messages of hope from those that felt a connection through my story.

Through all of this, I discovered that the more honest I became with myself, the more honest I became with others. For years I had performed strength, convinced that composure was the same as resilience. But real resilience required something softer. It required the truth. It required recognizing the fear, the anger, the exhaustion, and allowing those emotions to exist without letting them define me.

I began to notice that the more intentionally I focused on joy during the hard days, the steadier I felt. A deliberate choice to look at what remained instead of only what was missing. Grief had once narrowed my vision, and it trained my eyes to notice the absence. Joy required retraining them to recognize presence.

Anniversaries used to feel like something to brace for. The dates circled on the calendar carried weight long before they arrived. Over time, I decided I did not want those days to exist solely as reminders of loss. Now, on the anniversaries of my parents' passing and, on their birthdays, I try to pay something forward. I let their memory move outward instead of inward. A small act of kindness or a quiet generosity is a simple reminder that love can continue beyond the years we were given.

The shift from "why me" to "because of me" did not happen overnight. It unfolded slowly, with each passing year. I realized that the pain had shaped me, but it did not have to harden me. It could deepen me and widen my capacity for compassion. It could teach me to show up differently in the lives of others.

Several years ago, long before I understood this shift fully, I committed to walking in the Susan G. Komen 3-Day, 60 mile walk for breast cancer research. Not only did I finish the entirety of the three day walk once, but I continued to train, hold fundraisers, suffer through blisters and exhaustion for three consecutive years. By the end of it, more than $10,000 had been raised in honor of my mom.

At the time, I told myself I was simply participating in something meaningful. Looking back now, I understand it differently. Each mile was an answer to helplessness. Each step was a declaration that her story would not end in silence. I could not change what happened to her, but I could choose what happened because of her.

That walk did not replace all of my grief, and it did not make the fact that my mom is not here any easier. But it showed me that pain could push me, instead of pause me. It taught me that action relieved despair. It planted the earliest seeds of what would later become my decision to live outward instead of inward.

There is something powerful about interrupting a difficult day with intentional kindness. Buying coffee for someone in line behind you, leaving a note where a stranger might find it. Calling someone you have been thinking about instead of sending a quick text message and then putting your phone away.

These gestures are small and simple, but they ripple farther than we realize.

The harder the day feels, the more determined I am not to let it close in on me. I fight back not with anger, but with generosity. And every time I do, something inside me softens. The darkness does not completely disappear, but more light can be seen.

With every passing milestone life becomes a little brighter.

Somewhere in this shift, I found a passion for creating and writing. Shaping words into something that felt less chaotic than the thoughts inside my head. What began as scribbled reflections turned into intentional pages. Those pages are now a self-guided journal written by me. The goal behind the journal was to make it refillable with additional chapters being created to encourage others to keep your story going, because we all have a story inside. The journal became proof that my voice was still here.

There was a time when I believed strength meant enduring what happened to me. Now I understand that strength is choosing what happens next. It is showing up even when anxiety lingers in the background. It is standing in auditoriums and on stages, speaking even when your voice shakes. It is measured not by what I have survived, but by my willingness to remain present.

I do not know what chapters still lie ahead for me. Life has taught me not to assume that the next page will be easy or predictable. But I do know this, I am no longer afraid of turning it.

My mom didn't get the chance to keep writing her story. My dad didn't either.

But I do.

And so do you.

What is your story within?

About the Author

Abbey's life has been shaped by both profound loss and intentional renewal. After losing her mother to breast cancer as a child and her father in adulthood, she navigated deep grief, mental health challenges, and the complexities of blended family life. She did all this while pursuing her nursing career and raising seven children.

Through years of therapy, advocacy, and personal growth, Abbey found her voice through writing. What began as private journaling became a deeper calling to speak honestly about healing, prevention, and the quiet strength found in choosing to stay present. She is the creator of *A Story Within*, a self-guided journal rooted in her belief that every person carries a story worth honoring and continuing.

Abbey speaks openly about grief, faith, mental health, and the power of prevention, while encouraging others to advocate for themselves and live intentionally. Her faith has deepened through steady presence in small signs, quiet moments, and the courage to keep moving forward.

She lives with her husband, their seven children, and their dog, Harley, where life is busy, imperfect, and full of love. Her greatest work happens at home while around the dinner table, cheering on the sidelines, or in the small moments that shape a life. Beyond that she enjoys writing, speaking, traveling to the ocean, and working part-time as a nurse.

Dedication

To my husband: Thank you for choosing me and staying beside me. Thank you for walking through the hard years and for growing alongside me. Thank you for loving both the filtered and unfiltered versions of me.

To my children: You are my greatest gifts in life. I am endlessly proud of who you are and who you are becoming. As always, have a good day, be a good friend, and make good choices.

To Harley: Thank you for always being by my side, just as I needed. You came into my life as a form of therapy, and you have never let me down. I cherish every day we have together.

To my brothers: Mom and Dad gave us this life, I pray we live it to its fullest. We are pieces of who they were, and we are the ones that get to carry on their legacy.

To Jan, Steve, Anne, Ellen, and Aaron: Thank you for choosing and accepting me as your own. You gave me a place to land when I needed it most.

To my friends: Thank you for not just checking in, but actually showing up. You are the ones who didn't disappear when the world moved on.

To the doctors, nurse practitioners and therapists: Thank you for giving me a second chance of life. I couldn't have done it without you.

And, finally, to my mom and dad, Scott and Kay Henry: This book is for you. Not in grief, but in gratitude. You didn't get the chance at this life, but I did. And I am using it.